SOUTH HOLLAND PUBLIC LIBRARY

3 1350 00314 5713

DISCARD

D1544713

SOUTH HOLLAND PUBLIC LIBRARY

708/331-5262

M-Th. 10-9, Fri. 10-6, Sat. 10-5

www.southhollandlibrary.org

DISCARD

Celebrating Differences

We All Come from
Different Cultures

by **Melissa Higgins**

Consulting editor: Gail Saunders-Smith, PhD

Consultant: Donna Barkman
Children's Literature Specialist and Diversity Consultant
Ossining, New York

CAPSTONE PRESS
a capstone imprint

Pebble Plus is published by Capstone Press,
1710 Roe Crest Drive, North Mankato, Minnesota 56003.
www.capstonepub.com

Copyright © 2012 by Capstone Press, a Capstone imprint. All rights reserved.
No part of this publication may be reproduced in whole or in part, or stored in a retrieval system, or transmitted in any
form or by any means, electronic, mechanical, photocopying, recording, or otherwise, without written permission of the
publisher. For information regarding permission, write to Capstone Press,
1710 Roe Crest Drive, North Mankato, Minnesota 56003.

Books published by Capstone Press are manufactured with paper
containing at least 10 percent post-consumer waste.

Library of Congress Cataloging-in-Publication Data
Higgins, Melissa
 We all come from different cultures / by Melissa Higgins.
  p. cm.—(Pebble Plus. Celebrating differences)
 Includes bibliographical references and index.
 Summary: "Simple text and full-color photos explore and celebrate differences in cultures"—Provided by publisher.
 ISBN 978-1-4296-7577-2 (library binding)—ISBN 978-1-4296-7887-2 (paperback)
 1. Minorities—United States—Juvenile literature. 2. Multiculturalism—United States—Juvenile literature. I. Title.
E184.A1H487 2012
 305.800973—dc23   2011040397

3 1350 00314 5713   DISCARD

Editorial Credits
Jeni Wittrock, editor; Gene Bentdahl, designer; Svetlana Zhurkin, media researcher; Kathy McColley, production
   specialist; Marcy Morin, photo scheduler; Sarah Schuette, photo stylist

Photo Credits
Alamy: LHB Photo, 1; Capstone Studio: Karon Dubke, cover, 13; Dreamstime: Jose Gil, 8–9, Noam Armonn, 15;
Getty Images: Ariel Skelley, 21; iStockphoto: Christopher Futcher, 5, Coral Coolahan, 17; Photolibrary: Jian Chen, 6–7;
Shutterstock: Shestakoff, 18–19; Svetlana Zhurkin, 11

Note to Parents and Teachers

The Celebrating Differences series supports national social studies standards related to
individual development and identity. This book describes and illustrates differences in cultures.
The images support early readers in understanding the text. The repetition of words and
phrases helps early readers learn new words. This book also introduces early readers to subject-
specific vocabulary words, which are defined in the Glossary section. Early readers may need
assistance to read some words and to use the Table of Contents, Glossary, Read More, Internet
Sites, and Index sections of the book.

Printed in the United States of America in North Mankato, Minnesota.
102011   006405CGS12

Table of Contents

American and More

We are Americans
of all different cultures.
We have proud heritages
to share.

Celebrating Our Heritage

My parents came to America from Mexico. On the fifth day of every May, we celebrate a holiday called Cinco de Mayo.

LOS ANGELES / MEXICO CITY
SISTER CITIES

30th ANNIVERSARY
1969 - 1999

MAYOR RICHARD J. RIORDAN
MAYOR ROSARIO ROBLES-BERLANGA

7

Chinese New Year lasts
two weeks. A dancing dragon
and popping firecrackers bring
good luck to everyone.

A pavada is a dress

young girls wear in India.

I felt proud at my school's

Ethnic Celebration day.

My ancestors came from Africa

more than 200 years ago.

Our class made African animal

masks for Black History Month.

Sharing Customs

My best friend likes to eat
Middle Eastern lunch at
my house. Falafel pita
sandwiches are the best.

My Navajo grandmother
weaves beautiful wool rugs.
My favorite designs are
of the rain and of our
sacred mountains.

My name is Filippa.
In Swedish, that means
"someone who likes
horses." I love horses!

We Like Being Different

It's cool that our ancestors came from so many different places. It's even cooler that we all live in America together.

Glossary

ancestor—a family member who lived a long time ago

culture—a group of people's beliefs, customs, and way of life

ethnic—having to do with a group of people sharing the same language, traditions, and religion

falafel—a spicy patty made from vegetables and beans

heritage—history and traditions handed down from the past

Navajo—an American Indian group from the western United States

pita—a thin, flat bread that can be separated into layers to form a pocket

sacred—holy or deserving great respect

Read More

Adamson, Heather. *Families in Many Cultures.* Life around the World. Mankato, Minn.: Capstone Press, 2008.

Jules, Jacqueline. *Duck for Turkey Day.* Morton Grove, Ill.: Albert Whitman, 2009.

Leavitt, Caroline. *The Kids' Family Tree Book.* New York: Sterling Publ., 2007.

Internet Sites

FactHound offers a safe, fun way to find Internet sites related to this book. All of the sites on FactHound have been researched by our staff.

Here's all you do:

Visit *www.facthound.com*

Type in this code: 9781429675772

 **Super-cool stuff!** Check out projects, games and lots more at **www.capstonekids.com**

Index

Word Count: 164
Grade: 1
Early-Intervention Level: 20